DISCOVER THE
CONTINENTS

Antarctica

by Emily Rose Oachs

BLASTOFF!
READERS
3

BELLWETHER MEDIA • MINNEAPOLIS, MN

Note to Librarians, Teachers, and Parents:

Blastoff! Readers are carefully developed by literacy experts and combine standards-based content with developmentally appropriate text.

Level 1 provides the most support through repetition of high-frequency words, light text, predictable sentence patterns, and strong visual support.

Level 2 offers early readers a bit more challenge through varied simple sentences, increased text load, and less repetition of high-frequency words.

Level 3 advances early-fluent readers toward fluency through increased text and concept load, less reliance on visuals, longer sentences, and more literary language.

Level 4 builds reading stamina by providing more text per page, increased use of punctuation, greater variation in sentence patterns, and increasingly challenging vocabulary.

Level 5 encourages children to move from "learning to read" to "reading to learn" by providing even more text, varied writing styles, and less familiar topics.

Whichever book is right for your reader, Blastoff! Readers are the perfect books to build confidence and encourage a love of reading that will last a lifetime!

This edition first published in 2016 by Bellwether Media, Inc.

No part of this publication may be reproduced in whole or in part without written permission of the publisher. For information regarding permission, write to Bellwether Media, Inc., Attention: Permissions Department, 5357 Penn Avenue South, Minneapolis, MN 55419.

Library of Congress Cataloging-in-Publication Data

Oachs, Emily Rose.
  Antarctica / by Emily Rose Oachs.
      pages cm. – (Blastoff! Readers: Discover the Continents)
  Includes bibliographical references and index.
  Summary: "Simple text and full-color photography introduce beginning readers to Antarctica. Developed by literacy experts for students in kindergarten through third grade"– Provided by publisher.
  Audience: Grades K-3.
  ISBN 978-1-62617-324-8 (hardcover : alk. paper)
  1. Antarctica–Juvenile literature. 2. Antarctica–Geography–Juvenile literature. I. Title.
  G863.O23 2016
  919.89–dc23
                            2015028683

Printed in the United States of America, North Mankato, MN.

Table of Contents

The Coldest Continent

Antarctica is the coldest **continent**. On average, its high temperature is -49 degrees Fahrenheit (-45 degrees Celsius)!

DID YOU KNOW?

- Lake Vostok lies below ice that is more than 2 miles (3.2 kilometers) thick.

- At the South Pole, the sun does not set between September and March.

- If all of Antarctica's ice melted, the oceans would rise more than 200 feet (61 meters)!

- In 1983, the temperature in Antarctica dropped to -128.6 degrees Fahrenheit (-89.2 degrees Celsius)!

South Pole

Few people see Antarctica's **landmarks**. Some climb Mount Vinson, the tallest peak. Others journey to the **South Pole**.

Where Is Antarctica?

Antarctica is at the bottom of the globe. No other continent sits farther south.

Antarctica's land covers the South Pole. It lies in the Southern, Western, and Eastern **hemispheres**. The Southern Ocean surrounds the continent.

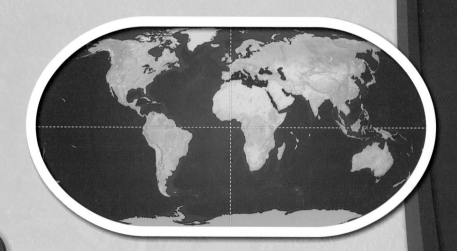

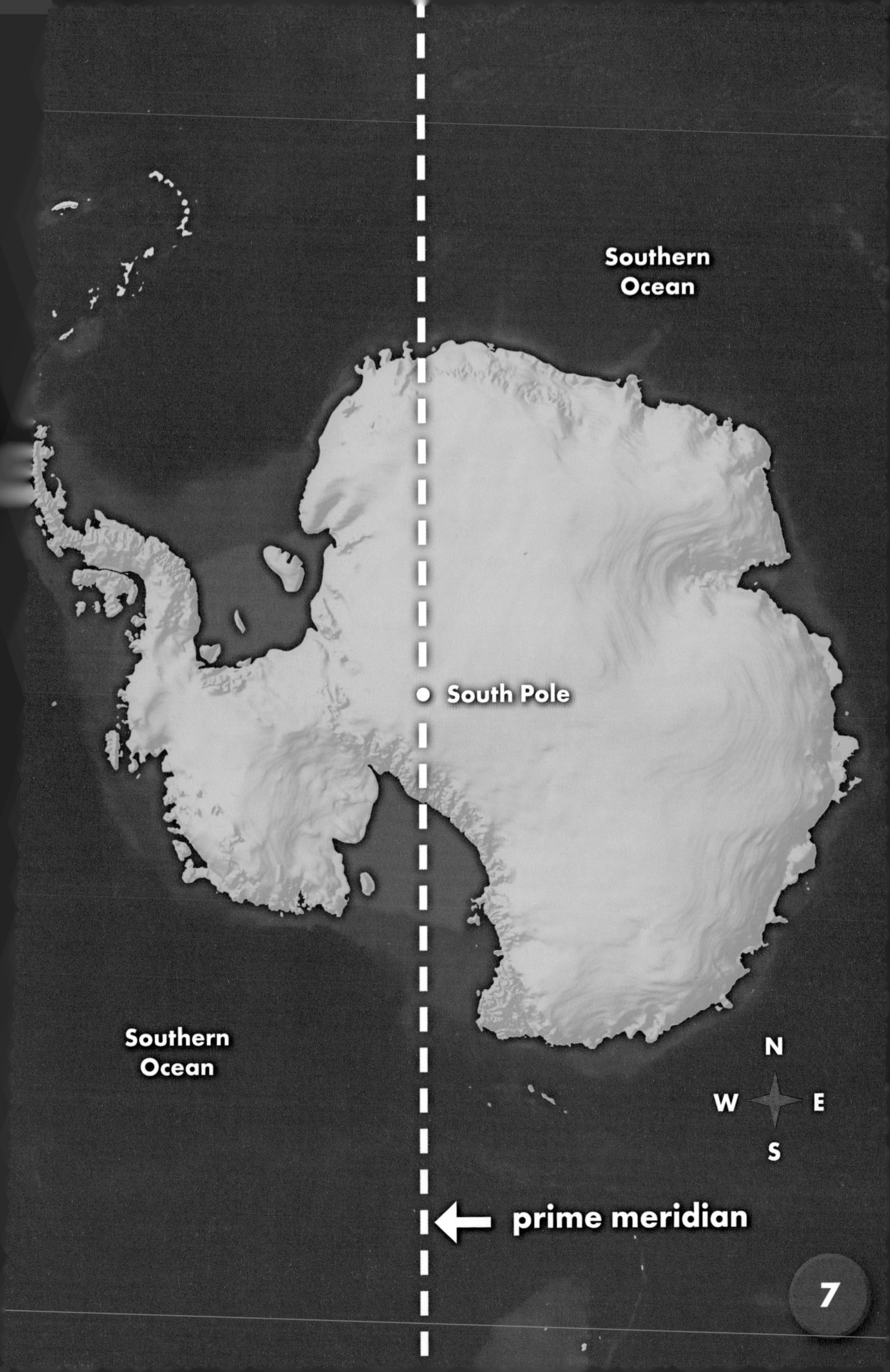

Southern
Ocean

South Pole

Southern
Ocean

N

W · E

S

← prime meridian

ice shelf

Huge **ice sheets** cover most of Antarctica. The ice can be almost 3 miles (4.8 kilometers) thick! **Ice shelves** reach beyond the coasts. Parts float on water.

Pieces of ice shelves may break off into the ocean. They become **icebergs**.

iceberg

Transantarctic
Mountains

The Transantarctic Mountains cross the continent. Buried beneath Antarctica's ice are valleys, lakes, and other mountains.

The Antarctic **Peninsula** reaches toward South America. It is Antarctica's warmest area. The inner part of the continent is colder than the coasts.

Antarctic
Peninsula

Transantarctic
Mountains

Antarctic
Peninsula

N
W   E
S

The Plants and Animals

moss

lichen

Few plants and animals can survive in Antarctica. Moss and **lichen** grow where there is no ice.

Only two kinds of flowering plants grow in Antarctica. Antarctic pearlwort and Antarctic hair grass bloom on the peninsula.

Antarctic pearlwort

Antarctic hair grass

Millions of penguins live along Antarctica's coast. In the ocean, they hunt for krill. Seals, squids, and octopuses also live in surrounding waters.

krill

seal

octopus

penguin

blue whale

Each summer, blue whales **migrate** to Antarctica's waters. They travel half the globe to find food.

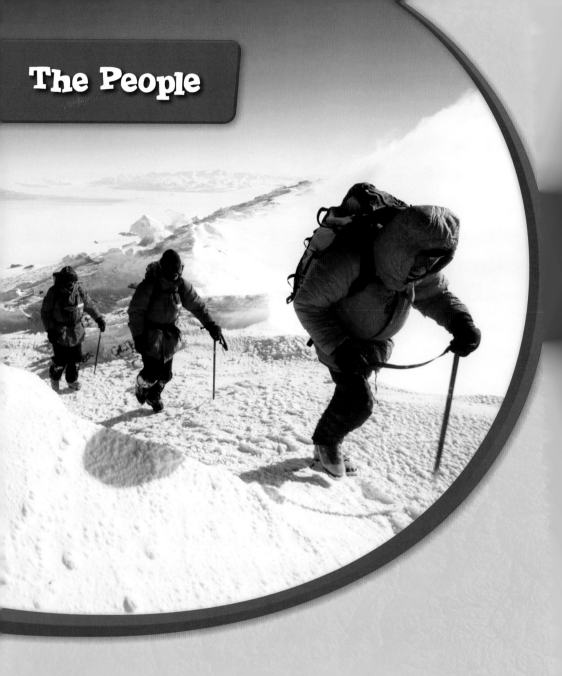

Antarctica does not have a permanent **population**. It is too cold for people to settle there.

In the summer, Antarctica's population reaches around 4,400 people. About 1,100 people live there in the winter. Most people on the continent are scientists.

McMurdo Station

Around 29 countries have **research bases** in Antarctica. The United States runs McMurdo Station, the largest. About 1,000 people live there in the summer.

People from around the world research together at McMurdo. Scientists use Antarctica to learn more about the planet.

Fast Facts About Antarctica

Size: 5.4 million square miles
(14 million square kilometers);
5th largest continent

Countries with Research Bases: 29

Number of People: 1,100 (winter);
4,400 (summer)

Place with Most People: McMurdo Station

Top Natural Resources: oil, coal, fish

Top Landmarks:
- Deception Island
- Mount Vinson
- South Pole
- Ross Ice Shelf

Deception
Island

Mount
Vinson

N
W ✦ E
S

McMurdo
Station

Ross
Ice Shelf

South Pole

Glossary

continent—one of the seven main land areas on Earth; the continents are Africa, Antarctica, Asia, Australia, Europe, North America, and South America.

hemispheres—halves of the globe; the equator and prime meridian divide Earth into different hemispheres.

ice sheets—large, thick areas of ice that cover a region

ice shelves—huge sheets of floating ice that are connected to land

icebergs—large pieces of floating ice in the ocean

landmarks—important structures or places

lichen—types of small plants that grow on rocks and walls

migrate—to travel from one place to another, often with the seasons

peninsula—a section of land that extends out from a larger piece of land and is almost completely surrounded by water

population—the number of people who live in an area

research bases—places where people gather information about something

South Pole—Earth's southernmost point

To Learn More

AT THE LIBRARY
Ganeri, Anita. *Introducing Antarctica*. Chicago, Ill.:
Capstone Heinemann Library, 2014.

London, Jonathan. *Little Penguin: The Emperor of
Antarctica*. New York, N.Y.: Marshall Cavendish
Children's, 2011.

Roza, Greg. *Mapping Antarctica*. New York, N.Y.:
Gareth Stevens Publishing, 2014.

ON THE WEB
Learning more about Antarctica
is as easy as 1, 2, 3.

1. Go to www.factsurfer.com.

2. Enter "Antarctica" into the search box.

3. Click the "Surf" button and you will see a
   list of related web sites.

With factsurfer.com, finding more
information is just a click away.

Index

The images in this book are reproduced through the courtesy of: Denis Burdin, front cover; Photodynamic, p. 4; Ann Hawthorne/ Corbis, p. 5; Paula Jones, p. 8; Biosphoto/ SuperStock, p. 9 (top); Juancat, p. 9 (bottom); Galen Rowell/ Corbis, p. 10; D. Parer &amp, E. Parer-Cook/ Pantheon/ SuperStock, p. 11; Gordon Wiltsie/ Getty Images, pp. 12 (top), 21 (top right); Maksym Deliyergiyev, p. 12 (bottom); Colin Harris/ era-images/ Alamy, p. 13 (top); Universal Images Group/ DeAgostini/ Alamy, p. 13 (bottom); Anton_Ivanov, p. 14 (top); Jean-Paul Ferrero/ ardea.com/ Pantheon/ SuperStock, p. 14 (top right); Volodymyr Goinyk, p. 14 (middle right); Norbert Wu/ SuperStock, p. 14 (bottom right); powell'sPoint, p. 15; George Steinmetz/ Corbis, p. 16; Vicinanza/ Newscom, p. 17; Martyn Unsworth, pp. 18-19; Maxily, p. 21 (top left); Tui De Roy/ Minden Pictures/ Corbis, p. 21 (bottom left); Darryn Schneider, p. 21 (bottom right).